Events Leading to the American Revolution

Linda R. Wade

ABDO
& Daughters

Visit us at
www.abdopub.com

Published by ABDO Publishing Company, 4940 Viking Drive, Edina, MN 55435.
Copyright ©2001 by Abdo Consulting Group, Inc. International copyrights
reserved in all countries. No part of this book may be reproduced in any form
without written permission from the publisher.

Printed in the United States.

Contributing Editor, Graphic Design, Illustrations: John Hamilton
Cover photo: John Hamilton
Interior photos: John Hamilton, p. 1, 4, 6, 13, 17, 21, 22, 25, 27, 31
Independence NHP, p. 11, 18, 20
American Antiquarian Society, p. 16
Boston Athenaeum, p. 19
John Carter Brown Library, p. 15
Library of Congress, p. 23, 28

Sources: Collins, Robert A. *The History of America.* New York: CLB
Publishing, 1993; Carter, Alden R. *The American Revolution: Colonies in
Revolt.* New York: Franklin Watts, 1988; Gay, Kathlyn. *Revolutionary War.*
New York: Twenty-First Century Books, A Division of Henry Holt and
Company, Inc., 1995; Grant, R. G. *The American Revolution.* New York:
Thomas Learning, 1995; Kent, Deborah. *America the Beautiful:* (series).
Chicago: Childrens Press, 1988; Lukes, Bonnie L. *World History Series: The
American Revolution.* San Diego: Lucent Books, 1996; Microsoft Encarta '97
Encyclopedia; Stewart, Gail. *The Revolutionary War.* San Diego: Lucent Books,
1991.

Library of Congress Cataloging–in–Publication Data

Wade, Linda R.
    Events leading to the American Revolution / Linda R. Wade
        p. cm. -- (The American Revolution)
    Includes index.
    ISBN 1-57765-153-7
    1. United States--History--Revolution, 1775-1783--Causes--Juvenile literature.
[1. United States--History--Revolution, 1775-1783--Causes.] I. Title.

E210 .W27 2001
973.3'11--dc21

                                        00--56905

CONTENTS

INTRODUCTION

In the mid-1700s, the country we know today as the United States was a very different place. Instead of 50 states, there were 13 English colonies. Before 1754, France owned much of the land west of the Appalachian Mountains. England claimed the east.

Then came the French and Indian War of 1754-1763. French soldiers, together with Native Americans, fought against British soldiers and American colonists. The war lasted until the British captured Quebec, Canada, in 1759. In the peace treaty of 1763,

An Iroquois Indian taking part in a reenactment of the Battle of Newtown.

France lost most of its territory in North America. Great Britain obtained all the land east of the Mississippi River, except for New Orleans.

Because of this long struggle for land and control, Britain found itself with a large war debt. The country's solution to this problem was to tax the 13 colonies. These taxes brought serious disagreements and, finally, another war—the war that would change North America forever.

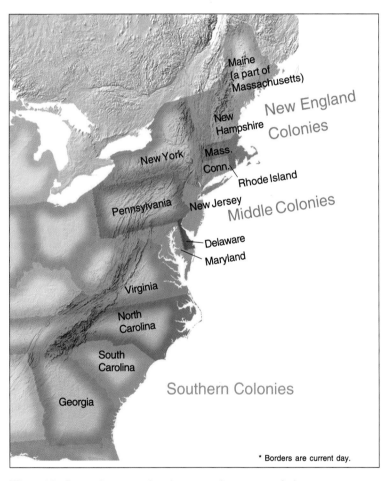

The 13 American colonies on the eve of the revolution.

Chapter 1

The Beginning Taxes

After the peace treaty with France was signed in 1763, the British government (Parliament) issued the Proclamation of 1763. This document said that the American colonists could not settle west of the Appalachian Mountains. The British thought this would keep peace with the Native Americans. The colonists objected to this ban.

The Appalachian Mountains.

They wanted to explore and go west to obtain land. While they liked being British, they wanted to set their own lifestyle.

The colonies in America were governed separately. Each had a governor who was appointed by the king of England. They were like independent countries, since each was started by a different set of people for different reasons (religious groups founded several of the colonies). Each colony imported and exported goods with the other colonies. Their common thread was that Great Britain claimed the land. Therefore, the British Parliament controlled all 13 colonies.

Meanwhile, Great Britain (often called England) was facing huge government debt because of its war with France. The country needed money. In fact, talk in the capital city of London centered on the possibility of the country going bankrupt.

With this in mind, Parliament decided that the American colonies should pay a part of the war costs. The colonies were prosperous. Their farms were producing, and the fishing industry was expanding. In addition, lumber from the American forests had become a big export item.

Parliament decided that it was only fair that the colonies share this abundance with their mother country. After all, even the American cities were growing. Philadelphia had a population of 40,000. The seacoast cities of New York, Boston, and Charleston, South Carolina, were growing. The Americans were happy and satisfied with their lives. They were content belonging to Great Britain.

In the American colonies, there were long-standing British laws that controlled trade. The colonies were allowed to buy and sell goods only to Britain. In reality, though, the colonists bypassed the English laws by smuggling, trading secretly with other European countries. Smuggling was important to the Americans, since no taxes had to be paid. Also there were no trade regulations on smuggled goods. This kept the prices lower so the people could buy what they needed.

Eventually, England's treasurer compared the amount of trade with the receipts, and soon realized that the colonists were smuggling goods. It was apparent that the customs officers were not doing their jobs, so he required them to keep exact accounts of imports and exports. In addition, English warships in American waters were allowed to seize smugglers. He even offered rewards.

Parliament was determined to get more money. They decided to tax certain items and services used by the colonists. In reality, these taxes were very small, only about $1.20 a year per person. But the colonists were angry. They did not want to give England any kind of tax.

The old Molasses Act of 1733 expired about this time. That act had placed a tax on molasses not produced in the British West Indies. Now it was modified, becoming the new Sugar Act of 1764. Even though it lowered the tax, the colonists thought it was still too high. The Currency Act added more taxes in 1764. This act said that the colonists had to pay the whole domestic debt created during the French and Indian War. Taxes on other imports were also raised. Foreign rum and French wines were banned entirely.

But what caused more outcries in the colonies was a British statement explaining the taxes. The purpose, the statement said, was to raise money in America "for defraying the expenses of defending, protecting, and securing" the colonies. Britain was 3,000 miles away. It took months to cross the ocean. The idea of being defended by Parliament seemed highly improbable to the colonists.

Major overseas
trade routes to and
from Boston.

To Boston: fish
To Newfoundland:
all goods

Boston

To Europe: raw materials / To Boston: manufactured goods

To Europe: raw materials

All goods

To Boston: slaves
To West Indies:
raw materials

To Africa: trade goods

To South America and West Indies: slaves and gold

CHAPTER 2

THE STAMP ACT

In 1765, the British Parliament issued the Stamp Act. It carried that name because an official stamp was required on items that affected everyone. These items included legal documents like marriage licenses and wills. Newspapers, playing cards, and anything printed on paper in the colonies needed a stamp before it could be sold. American merchants had to purchase stamps from official agents and put them on their goods.

Because most colonists thought these taxes were very unfair, protests erupted. In Connecticut, a lawyer named Jared Ingersoll accepted the position of stamp distributor. The people called him a traitor and hanged him in effigy. (A mob of protesters hanged a dummy dressed to look like Ingersoll.) A patriotic society called the Sons of Liberty was soon born. These radicals declared, "We will oppose the (Stamp Act) to the last extremity, even to take the field."

This great uproar spread to the other colonies. Merchants argued that they were not consulted before being required to purchase the stamps. Now they had to raise their prices to pay for the stamps. The colonists refused to buy any product that required a stamp. The boycott was so effective that commerce between Great Britain and America came to a halt.

In Virginia, Patrick Henry made a speech that became a theme of resistance. He said that colonists would accept taxation only if their elected representatives imposed it. This meant that the colonists would have to send delegates to Parliament. The famous cry of "No taxation without representation" came from Henry's speech.

At a town meeting in Braintree (now Quincy), Massachusetts, a young lawyer named John Adams also excited the colonists. He repeated the theme that taxation without representation was wrong. He encouraged the colonists to continue the boycott. They must do all they could, he said, to let Britain know that Americans were not puppets.

When King George learned of the unrest, he asked Parliament to remove the law. In March 1766, the Stamp Act was repealed.

The owner of the Pennsylvania Journal and Weekly Advertiser newspaper stopped publishing on October 31, 1765, because of the Stamp Act. "Adieu (good-bye) adieu to the Liberty of the Press," he wrote.

CHAPTER 3

THE TOWNSHEND ACTS

Even though the Stamp Act had failed to raise needed funds for England, the British government found another way to raise money. This time they created the Townshend Acts. Now the Americans would have to pay taxes on paper, paint, glass, lead, and tea. The money raised was supposed to be used to pay British officials in the American service.

As the colonists talked they began to realize that they had no say in any of the demands made by Britain. It was not fair. They were being taxed and could do little about it. They needed to be heard in Parliament. Each passing day reinforced their lack of representation in Parliament. Yet, many realized that even if they were present in Parliament, they would be voted down. Still, the cry of "no taxation without representation!" rang throughout the colonies.

When news of this commotion reached King George, he was very angry. Never before had colonies demanded rights for themselves. The British felt that the colonists' first duty was to Britain. The colonists did not agree. This disagreement would only get worse.

Another boycott was announced. Radicals urged the colonists to only buy items not listed in the Townshend Acts.

The colonies began to find strength in working together. The Massachusetts legislature sent a letter condemning the Townshend Acts. The letter also called for a united American resistance to the British taxation. Only Pennsylvania refused to join the alliance.

To fight the Townshend Acts, Americans were urged not to buy British goods, but to instead buy goods from local manufacturers. Not only would this hurt British merchants, it was hoped that buying American goods would make the colonies more self-sufficient.

CHAPTER 4

THE LOYALISTS

Not all of the American colonists agreed with the boycott of English goods. Some were still willing to stay loyal to the British government regardless of the various taxes. These people were called "loyalists" or "Tories." Most Tories wanted to see change, but a peaceful one. They wanted to remain within the British government.

Some communities treated the Loyalists with disrespect. In Connecticut the colonists made life very difficult for the Tories. They took away their land and belongings and drove them out of the colony.

In other places Loyalists were kidnapped and covered with tar and feathers. Then they were put out for public display.

Many families became divided. In one Georgia family, James Habersham, a wealthy partner in Georgia's oldest house of commerce, remained loyal to the king. His three sons all became radical patriots. This kind of family division happened throughout the colonies. Even Benjamin Franklin's son William, remained true to England while Benjamin was a patriot.

News of the continuing restlessness in America drifted back to England. British officials decided to send more soldiers to the 13 colonies to put an end to the unrest.

The tarring and feathering of a loyalist in Boston.

CHAPTER 5

BOSTON INVASION

Late in September, 1768, 4,000 British soldiers (sometimes called "redcoats") invaded Boston harbor and occupied the city. These soldiers were not welcome by the citizens.

The soldiers took over a church, and some decided to live there. They even rode their horses in the church. That kind of behavior greatly angered the colonists.

Americans did not want the British laws. They did not want the taxes. And, they certainly did not need the British army to maintain the peace.

British troops land at Boston's Long Warf in 1768.

British troops were unwelcome by most Boston residents.

All the unrest brought on by the British only increased the determination of the patriots to work together. Alone they could do little, but as a united people, they could approach Parliament with demands.

By the autumn of 1769, the boycott was showing its effectiveness. People were not buying luxury items such as expensive alcoholic beverages, sugar, pewter, hats, and shoes. English exports to America dropped by one third.

By 1770, Parliament had repealed the taxes on everything except tea. King George III kept the tax on tea to prove that England was still in control.

But trouble was brewing throughout the colonies. Citizens were rebelling at the thought of their rights being taken away. There was uneasiness spreading through the people.

CHAPTER 6

THE BOSTON MASSACRE

March 5, 1770, was a cold, snowy day. A squad of British soldiers was patrolling the streets of Boston. About 50 or 60 angry colonists gathered to harass the soldiers. Even children teased them for their bright red uniforms. They called them "redcoats," and "lobster-backs."

The British paid no attention for a while, but finally, they got tired of being called nasty names. A shouting match between the two sides turned into a near-riot. Some Bostonians began throwing rocks. Others pelted the soldiers with snowballs and chunks of ice. Captain Thomas Preston tried to calm his British soldiers.

Suddenly gunfire rang out. Within a few seconds, five colonists lay dead in the street. One was a black man named Crispus Attucks, one of the first to die in the struggle for independence. Six more men were severely wounded.

Crispus Attucks was one of five killed at the Boston Massacre. Attucks was an African American sailor who had earlier escaped slavery.

Paul Revere's print of the Boston Massacre.

At least 10,000 persons watched the funeral processions of the five dead men. Shops and stores of Boston and neighboring towns closed. Church bells tolled.

The angry citizens of Boston demanded that the British troops leave their city. They also wanted a trial of the British officer. Captain Preston and his men were charged with murder. However, since no one could prove that Preston had ordered his men to fire, he was acquitted.

CHAPTER 7

OPPOSITION INCREASES

Samuel Adams, a radical who strongly opposed the British, was one of the colonists who took action. He was quick to arouse the people of Boston to oppose the British. He also realized that the fight against the British had to be waged in all the colonies, not just in Massachusetts. Adams persuaded the members of Boston's Town Meeting to set up a Committee of Correspondence. These committee members wrote to leaders in other colonies and encouraged them to coordinate protest groups. He said the colonists must work together.

Samuel Adams.

Samuel Adams also wrote pamphlets that stirred the people. He made what many thought of as a simple street fight into a deliberate slaughter (the Boston Massacre). He knew how to excite people with his words.

Paul Revere was also considered a radical. He worked with Adams by drawing a picture of British troops coldly firing on an unarmed and seemingly innocent gathering of people.

All of this stirred the people. Parliament realized that things were getting out of control in America. They knew they had to improve the situation.

The first thing they did was repeal the Townshend Acts. The only exception was the tax on tea. England wanted to prove that it still had the power to tax the colonies. This was aggravating to the colonists; tea was their favorite beverage. However, for three years they lived with the tea tax.

The British still needed money, and the colonies continued to be the best source of revenue. In May 1773, Parliament passed another act that angered colonists even more. The British East India Company was given a monopoly on tea. This meant that only the East India Company could sell tea to the colonies. They sold it without paying any of the import duties. Since no import taxes were charged, this tea actually cost less.

By this time, the people did not care about the price. They were afraid of monopolies. Merchants worried that Parliament might establish other monopolies and drive the Americans out of business. The colonists feared that eventually monopolies would actually drive the prices up and exploit the people.

Opposition leaders often communicated with the public by printing pamphlets and newspapers on printing presses like this one at Franklin Court in Philadelphia.

CHAPTER 8

THE BOSTON TEA PARTY

The colonists in Boston met and decided that something must be done about the tax on tea. When three ships came into the Boston Harbor loaded with tea, the colonists refused to let it be unloaded. The British government then said that they would unload the tea under the protection of cannons and guns.

On December 16, 1773, Samuel Adams and the Sons of Liberty held a big meeting. Fiery speeches were made. Afterwards, about

A replica of the *Beaver*, a ship plundered during the Boston Tea Party, now rests in Boston Harbor as a floating museum.

Colonists, some disguised as Mohawk Indians, dump British tea into Boston Harbor.

100 men stormed out of the meeting. Disguised as Mohawk Indians, they slipped away to the harbor. Once there, they divided into three groups. Each group was assigned to a ship. Quickly and quietly, they boarded the ships that held the tea. They faced the captains and forced them below. Then the Americans pulled the tea to the edge of the ship. They took their hatchets and chopped open the chests of tea. Splash! The tea was gone. They had dumped it into the water.

It took just over two hours to destroy 342 chests of tea. Adams realized that all the colonies must be notified of this event. He sent Paul Revere to spread the word.

Newspapers quickly printed the story. They called it the "Boston Tea Party." Radicals everywhere cheered the Sons of Liberty.

CHAPTER 9

PARLIAMENT REACTS

The British government was furious when it learned of the Boston Tea Party. Parliament and King George III were determined to punish the colonists.

By the following spring, Britain's plan was in place. Since shipping through the port of Boston was so important to the colonies, the English decided to shut it down. No ships could go in or out of the port until the city paid for the tea that had been dumped.

Britain's King George III.

Parliament even did away with the elected assembly of Massachusetts. A British general, Thomas Gage, became the governor. No town meetings could be held without his approval. General Gage received orders to arrest Adams. However, the British failed to capture him.

Parliament then forced Boston residents to house and feed the British soldiers stationed there. The Americans even had to buy blankets and rum for the soldiers. This was called the Quartering

Act. The Americans found these new rules almost impossible to accept. They called these laws the Intolerable Acts.

It was obvious that most members of Parliament assumed that America and England were two different countries. Americans were considered inferior and irresponsible. If the Americans refused to accept their punishment, perhaps force would make them obey.

Because of the Quartering Act, American citizens were forced to house and feed British troops. The Americans hated this so much they called it the Intolerable Act.

CHAPTER 10

THE COLONISTS UNITE

With the Port of Boston closed, the people wondered how they would survive. Then food, clothing, fuel, and money began arriving from the other colonies. People in the other colonies thought that the people of Boston were suffering in the common cause of America.

In September 1774, 55 delegates chosen by committees in 12 states met in Philadelphia to discuss how to resist British tyranny. Only Georgia was not a part of the First Continental Congress.

The delegates developed a statement of rights, then sent a petition to Parliament. They did not seek independence from Great Britain; they only wanted to define the rights of the American colonists. They wanted an agreement that would eliminate the current problems. They said:

1. People have a right to life, liberty, and property.
2. People have a right to trial by jury.
3. People have the right to make laws in their own assemblies.
4. People have the right not to have soldiers living in their homes.

The Continental Congress also voted another boycott of British goods. Americans were asked not to use British products. They were also asked not to sell anything to the British.

Carpenter's Hall in Philadelphia, the site where the First
Continental Congress met in 1774.

CHAPTER 11

CONCLUSION

In most of the colonies it was feared that the Americans and the British would end up fighting each other. Patrick Henry stood before the Virginia House of Burgesses and made his famous speech. He said: "Is life so dear, or peace so sweet, as to be purchased at the price of chains and slavery? Forbid it, Almighty God! I know not what course others may take; but as for me, give me liberty or give me death!"

The time had come. Great Britain had to stop intruding into the lives of the colonists. These people were on free soil. They had become Americans. If necessary, they would fight to protect their rights and freedoms.

During his famous speech in front of the Virginia House of Burgesses, Patrick Henry said, "Give me liberty, or give me death!"

INTERNET SITES

ushistory.org
http://www.ushistory.org/

This Internet exploration of the Revolutionary War is presented by the Independence Hall Association. Visitors can learn interesting facts about many aspects of the war, including major battles, biographies of important patriots (Ben Franklin, Betsy Ross, Thomas Paine, and others), plus info on historic sites that can be toured today. The section on the Declaration of Independence includes photos of the document, as well as bios of the signers and Jefferson's account of the writing.

Liberty! The American Revolution
http://www.pbs.org/ktca/liberty/

The official online companion to "Liberty! The American Revolution," a series of documentaries originally broadcast on PBS in 1997. Includes timelines, resource material, and related topics—a potpourri of information on the American Revolution. Topics cover daily life in the colonies, the global village, a military point of view, plus a section on the making of the TV series. Also includes a "Revolutionary Game."

These sites are subject to change. Go to your favorite search engine and type in "American Revolution" for more sites.

PASS IT ON

American Revolutionary War buffs: educate readers around the country by passing on interesting information you've learned about the American Revolution. Maybe your family visited a famous Revolutionary War battle site, or you've taken part in a reenactment. Who's your favorite historical figure from the Revolutionary War? We want to hear from you!

To get posted on the ABDO Publishing Company Web site, email us at "History@abdopub.com"

Visit the ABDO Publishing Company Web site at www.abdopub.com

GLOSSARY

Boycott

A refusal to buy something in order to show disapproval.

Colony

A group of people who settle in a distant territory but remain citizens of their native country.

Loyalists

People who stayed loyal to Great Britain during the American Revolution.

Massacre

The killing of a large number of people who cannot defend themselves.

Monopoly

Complete control over a product or service.

Parliament

The law-making body of Great Britain.

Radicals

Colonists who were strongly opposed to the policies of the British.

Redcoats

The name that was often given to British soldiers because part of their uniform was a bright red coat.

Repeal

To withdraw or cancel.

Revolution

A large, sudden, change in government.

Sons of Liberty

A group of patriotic colonists who banded together to oppose the Stamp Tax, Townshend Acts, and other oppressing acts imposed by Great Britain.

Smuggle

To bring into or take out of a country secretly without paying legal duties.

Tories

A name applied to Loyalists who stayed true to Great Britain.

Tyranny

A harsh and unjust rule.

Philadelphia's Independence Hall.

INDEX

The Boston Tea Party.